Mr. Noisy

**Mr. Noisy made noise
when he walked.**

Mr. Noisy made noise
when he talked.

Mr. Noisy made noise
when he danced.

**Mr. Noisy made noise
when he sang.**

**Mr. Noisy made noise
when he drove his car.**

**Mr. Noisy made noise
when he rode his bike.**

"It's too noisy!" everybody yelled.

Mr. Noisy walked quietly.

Mr. Noisy talked quietly.

Mr. Noisy danced quietly.

Mr. Noisy sang quietly.
Mr. Noisy drove his car quietly.

Mr. Noisy rode his bike quietly.

"It's too quiet!" everybody yelled.
"Where's Mr. Noisy?"

"Here I am!"